SELF-C0ACHING
WITH
POWER TOOLS FOR
POWER PEOPLE

By

DR. BRENDA HATTINGH

PUBLISHED BY
CURRENCY COMMUNICATIONS (Pty Ltd)
Johannesburg, South Africa.

ISBN: 9798709210257

Cover design by Zander Hattingh
Editing by Copy-Writing: Quality Writing and Editing Services
Website: http://www.copy-writing.co.za;
Email: david.barraclough@copy-writing.co.za
Graphics by: Gerart Snyman
Email: info@gerart.co.za

Cover photo from Shuttertstock.

Published by:
Currency Communications International. (Pty. Ltd.)
Johannesburg. South Africa.

For more books in this series

Kindle and paperbacks available from:
Amazon books.www.amazon.com/author/brendahattingh
For more information email: info@powerintelligence.net .

**Authenticity is the daily practice
of letting go of who we think
we're supposed to be
and embracing who we are.**
Brene Brown

ABOUT THIS BOOK

The era of authenticity is here to stay. Our challenge is to think on our feet. Learning to coach yourself is a must if you want to secure a safe transition into a new level of human awareness and functioning while creating the life you want and desire.

In the series *'Authentic Living and Leading,'* we cover all the necessary information, skills, and tools you will need to coach yourself to a new level of health, wealth, happiness, and success.

In this starter package, you receive an E-book outlining how to identify the influence of your authentic self, versus your shadow ego-self. One side leads to success, while the other side leads to self-destruction.

You also receive daily *Power Tools for Power People* delivered to your inbox. Available here Your Daily Power Tools for Power People are available on our website. www.brendahattingh.com..

This starter package aims to help you redefine who you are, how to access your real power and potential while reclaiming your DNA success-blueprint. You were born to be successful and happy. It is in your DNA.

You need not settle for anything less.

SELF-COACHING

Background

As our current systems rapidly disintegrate and the new season of human consciousness emerges, the challenge to still stay connected, centred, grounded, and focused while developing a new quality of life becomes increasingly more demanding – even daunting.

The COVID-19 pandemic has taught us to think on our feet. One of our challenges is to learn how to coach ourselves.

This calls for a whole new mindset, skills, tools, and a new manual or script, for quality living.

Authenticity is here to stay

The season of authenticity is here to stay. This can and will challenge every person to rethink their value and belief systems, including their emotional, mental, social, religious, and financial programming while redefining success and prosperity.

Our challenge is to upgrade to a whole new approach to success, prosperity, happiness, and what a quality life really means. Some will be able to make this leap, while others will stay behind.[1]

This we all find within the self – the authentic self. The authentic self[2] is that part of self that holds the keys to a happy, successful, fulfilling, and quality life. It is encoded as your DNA-blueprint.

Lost the plot.

Unfortunately, we became disconnected from this part of the self. We lost the plot and developed a shadow ego-self. This part of self has taken control of the lives of the multitudes. It flourishes on lies, deception, delusion, half and untruths, darkness, and negativity, and causes self-destruction. Unfortunately, most people have given their power away, lost sight of who they are, and are divorced from real success, happiness, and the truth about what they are truly capable of. This means most people have settled for mediocrity, struggle, and survival.

This is currently humanity's default setting.

The new energy of 2021

While 2020 brought a wake-up call in the form of the COVID-19 pandemic, 2021 introduces a new kind of energy. The year 2021 demands that each person remains mindful, conscious, and aware of the choices we need to make.

The choices are, or we stay where we are – or – we take the leap into a whole new future of health, wealth, happiness, and prosperity.

It is time to recover our original DNA success-blueprint. To achieve this level of success, we not only need a whole new mindset and heart-set, but we also need new power tools and skills.

Power Tools for Power People has been written for you and everyone else who chooses to take this leap of self-fulfillment while embarking on this exciting adventure.

One of the goals of this journey is to recover your true power and become successful, happy, and fulfilled.

However, we have to coach ourselves to get to this level.

Self-coaching

By consciously upgrading our level of self-knowledge, understanding, and self-mastery, we can overcome the shadow ego-self while connecting to the authentic self.

We can do this by learning how to coach ourselves.

We can cancel out and nullify the negative influence and social, educational, religious programming. We are awakening and becoming aware of the destructive force of the shadow ego-self, in the self and others. It is becoming clear how the ego uses power games to get what it wants. This includes manipulation, intimidation and interrogation, emotional dramas, being aloof, procrastination, retraction, passivity, and even depression.

Our challenge is to coach the self by securing and maintaining the new vibe of honesty, truth, integrity, and success. We need to maintain our power position. This is the level of self-mastery.

The right use of power

An important universal law we all need to adhere to is 'The right use of power or life force'. The power games the shadow ego-self uses, are nothing less than the abuse of power – or life force.

In the end, this all leads to self-destruction.

Happiness and the 'right use of power'.

When we take back our power from poor, loveless, destructive investments, we become happy and fulfilled. Only by understanding who the authentic self is, what authentic success and quality living mean.

By implementing new power tools and skills, we can begin to flourish and be prosperous.

So, being happy is the outcome of 'the right use of power'. This power is our daily life force or energy.

Our life force needs to be constantly replenished. We need new power tools that will give us a daily boost forward. Only then can we really meet our goals and fulfill our wants, needs, and desires, without depleting our energy resources.

Our challenge is to constantly fill up our reserves, just like our motor vehicles.

The purpose of this book

The purpose of the book is to provide powerful tools for people who have chosen and made the commitment to live in higher awareness and lead empowered lives, therefore the title *Power Tools for Power People*.

These tools were taken from the list of emotional and motivational tools outlined in the book *Power Intelligence: Mastering your miracle mind.* [3]

To move

The words 'emotion' and 'motivation' both come from the same Latin root word *movĕre* meaning 'to move'. Where 'emotions' (*e-movĕre*) means providing the 'energy to move', motives or 'motivation' provides the direction in which we need to move. These two principles provide a powerful unified force that can boost us forward if we are prepared to consciously harness this personal power.

First, we need to ask the question, who coaches who?

If you are familiar with the series 'Authentic Living and leading', you will by now know we have two sides of ourselves. On the one side, we find the real-me authentic self. On the other side, we have a disconnected, shadow ego-self. These two sides of self are mutually exclusive and in a constant battle for control in our lives. Whoever wins the battle determines the quality of your life.

Coaching yourself is all about mindfully overcoming the shadow ego-self by using your *daily Power Tools for Power People*. Here is a short overview of these two sides of self for those who have not yet read the book *'The Authentic Self. Coaching yourself to ultimate Success.'*[4]

The shadow ego-self

Each of us has parts of the self that have been disconnected, splintered, or 'broken off'. This disconnection is evident right down to a DNA level.[5] We find potential we have not yet discovered, identified with, connected to, grown, developed, or evolved, in these fragmented areas.

This means parts of us are still on the dark or shadow side. Unfortunately, most people live from a fragmented or broken disconnected self. This is the reason why the world is in the state that it is.

- **Being stuck**

These parts are still 'stuck' somewhere in the past and are constantly invading our lives to be heard, acknowledged, and resolved. This reflects in the many fragmented and unhappy lives around us.

Most people neglect to reincorporate the fragments and learn from their shadow self.

This happens mostly because we are – or unaware or ashamed of these parts that are not 'up to standard'. We rather choose to deny and ignore their existence. This drains much of our personal power and prevents us from moving forward.

• Becoming unstuck

However, connecting to and taking conscious control of the shadow self, is a very valuable step in becoming unstuck. By reclaiming your power, you can grow in self-coaching, mastery, and maturity. If not, the shadow ego-self will continue to dominate your personal dynamics while influencing your life negatively and destructively.

• Stop signs

At some time or other – everyone needs to stop and take personal control and responsibility for the quality of their lives. Stop signs come in different forms and sizes.

We find the three main signals that something needs to change as problems with relationships, finances, and health. Sometimes we can face problems in all three of these areas of our lives, at the same time.

The more you ignore the signals, the loader, and more severe the call to action becomes.

Once we decide to stop, take a deep breath, and choose to face the real issues at hand, we can take control. We also need to face our shadow side and consciously open up, expose, and heal our negative aspects. Unfortunately, the shadow ego-self resists these efforts.

• Sabotage

It will sabotage everything you do to minimize any attempt to expose and nullify its hold on you, your thought processes, emotional dynamics, beliefs, and value system.

However, if we persevere, we can consciously reconnect to the healed, whole, holy, original, authentic self. At the same time, our DNA success-blueprint reconnects as well releasing a power surge that propels us forward. . We not only take back our power, but we also reclaim our authentic spark of life.

The authentic self

The terms 'original', 'authentic', 'real', 'higher' or 'soul' self[6'] are used interchangeably. This refers to the spiritual, light, or higher aspects of the individual self.

Jung considered 'individuation' as a psychological process of integrating the opposites of self. It also includes integrating the conscious with the unconscious mind while still maintaining relative autonomy. These are all necessary and important steps for a person to become healed, whole, 'holy' and One.

- **Universal Self**

The 'authentic self' is the whole self, the healed self, the 'whole integrated self', the Holy self. At the same time our authentic self is connected to and one with the universal cosmic web of life, higher consciousness, one-mind, or God-self.

Here we connect to the awareness of ourselves as a unique authentic spiritual soul-person or individual.[7]. At a universal level, we are part of the Universal Self.

We also are part of the Divine Universe or, 'one-song'. We are therefore also a being of light and a 'note', a sound or word of truth, in the symphony we call Creation. We were called into existence by the Creator.

Just as the song needs the notes, the notes need the song. One can only find meaningful self-expression as part of the harmony with the Oneness. All this takes place on different wavelengths, frequencies, or 'rays of light'. Because we resonate at different levels, we attract different people, things, and situations into our life, according to the level we function on.

- **Our unique imprint**

As a multi-dimensional spiritual light being, we have the opportunity and potential to make a personal unique light imprint on the fabric of life.

By living in this conscious awareness of the power of the authentic self, we can co-create miracles. We were created to live 'happily ever after' by just being our authentic self in everything we do.

This gives substance and meaning to our existence, not only in physical reality but also on higher planes.[8]

• **Became disconnected**

We lost this ability because we became disconnected, forgot who we are, were derailed, and started living according to the programming and brainwashing of lower frequency influences.

Humanity lost consciousness, became mindless while living meaningless, self-destructive lives. We started living from our unsound or insane minds and created the insane illusion we call the ego-reality.

In the end, we not only forgot our authentic self, but we also became enslaved by the lower ego-self and all the trappings it includes. In short – we 'fell from grace'.

A few questions remain. *Where is the authentic self? What does it look like and how do we get reconnected and remember?*

• **Spiritual children**

The authentic self is where it has always been and will always remain – on the higher, spiritual planes.[9] We are spiritual children of the Creator. It is the immaculate and pure concept, the perfect blueprint or 'whole image' of the soul, held by the universal mind of Source – God. Our original blueprint remains in universal consciousness – the heart of God.

As a spiritual light being, the authentic self is cosmic light[10] with a unique light imprint, unique sound, tone and resonance, and a unique personal individual quality.

Although it is unique and individual it only becomes meaningful when it is expressed as part of the Divine Matrix, Oneness, body of Christ. This is the whole-self or holy self. This is who we authentically are.

- ## Becoming conscious

The challenge is first to become conscious of and disconnect from the delusional ego-driven self with all its lies, misconceptions, and half-truths of who we authentically are. We need to see the liar, the plagiarist for what it is. Our challenge is to become aware of the fear, negativity, and darkness the shadow ego-self represents.

We can disconnect from lower dark frequencies and the negative influence in our lives, by consciously raising our awareness, changing our resonance, and accessing new levels of consciousness. By cleaning up and cleaning out our physical body, mind, soul, and spiritual selves, we can detox and detangle from the old.

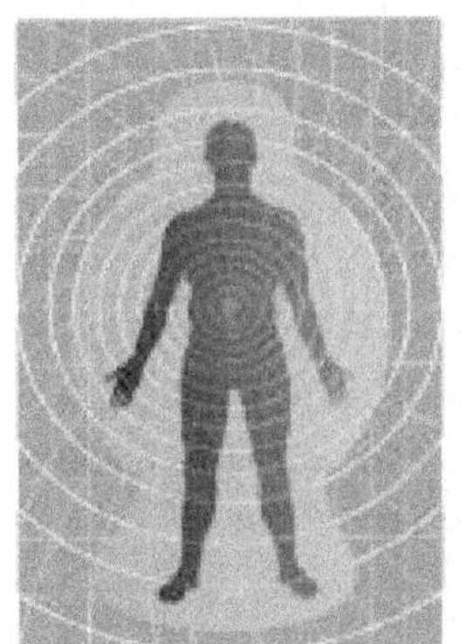
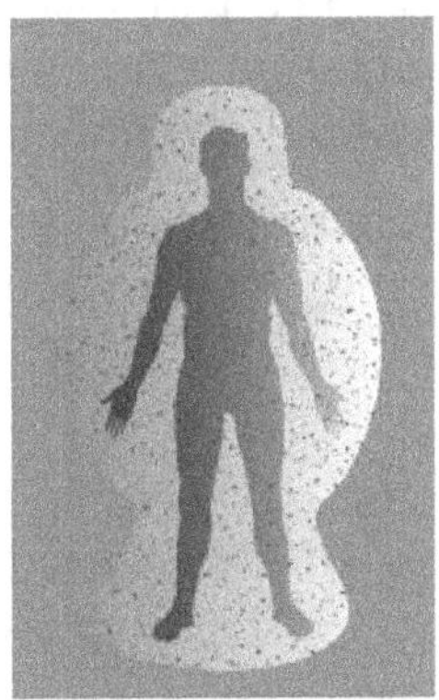

Open authentic self.   **Closed, shadow ego-self**

We have the power to reclaim our authentic self and all it stands for.

In essence, we have to be 're-born' into our new self and a new consciousness of quality of life and living. In this process our junk-genes become re-connected, emitting new light.

We start to resonate on a new frequency and can access higher planes.

Resonating with the song of love

We begin to resonate with a new note as part of the song of the Universe. This is the song of love. Here we reconnect with universal love, the Love Law, and align our body, mind, soul, spirit, and all our energies with the frequency of love.[11]

Our next challenge is to love the authentic self. Falling in love with our higher soul self is one of our most challenging experiences up to date. The reason is that the shadow ego-self will try to sabotage everything you do. The ego-self will even try to demotivate you to use this book and your daily power tools. It will even try to convince you of the lie, untruths, half-truths while trying to sabotage every new thought, value, and emotion that could cause its demise. So, be forewarned.

However, once you connect to peace, love, compassion, and understanding, you can see the delusion for what it is. You begin to love yourself. Then, and only then, can we love others as ourselves.

In the process, we also find our way home – back to Source. In the process, we also learn to co-create miracles.

Creating happiness

By accepting responsibility for and taking ownership of our life, our mental programming, emotional reactions, and the way we manage life and master the self, we also release new energy and powerful life force.

This propels us forward while providing the energy necessary to meet our goals, and fulfill our dreams, desires, needs, and wants. This makes us happy. This means that at the same time this can also be used as a 'happiness scale'.

The truth is that no-one can make you happy. Others can only make you less unhappy. We all need to create our happiness – and then share it with others.

A new baseline

Currently, we are experiencing an explosion of positivity that is now becoming available in different forms. This means that the foundation for creating health, wealth, and happiness is now moving from the dark, shadow-driven ego-self that is destructive - to a new constructive, positive foundation that is based on universal values, health, wealth, truth, honesty, integrity, and authentic self-expression.

 Our baseline of human functioning is shifting as we speak. We are moving from struggle and survival to flow and the freedom to create our reality. How to shift your emotional baseline is outlined in the book *Power Intelligence*.[12]

Daily Power Tools

The aim of this book, *Power Tools for Power People*, is to provide a daily power tool that will keep you going while you consciously take back your power; overcome, heal, or 'sacrifice' your ego-self, and master and develop the light or authentic self.

At the same time, these power tools are meant not only to boost your self-coaching, personal mastery, but also to provide insight into the thoughts, actions, and emotional baselines that other people function on.

With this new awareness and deeper understanding, we can consciously manage and even rise above their destructive patterns and power games. By being mindful we can stay out of the downdraught they cause. This demands a high level of awareness and self-mastery. This is how authentic leaders with an enabled DNA leadership-blueprint,

These enlightened leaders know that their tasks are to set the standards, mark the boundaries, benchmark the qualities, highlight the values, and outline the path from delusion into truth, honesty, integrity, and enlightenment.

This is how we all should show the way out of this dark, depressing life of self-destruction. This is also the task of the alchemist. This is also our task when we embark on this path of authenticity.

The alchemist

An alchemist is a person who is committed to changing lower-order human potential into higher-order human power. This also includes a spiritual journey.

The question is: how do e become an all-important 'alchemist'?

- **People are waking up**

Humanity as *Homo sapiens* is the only species on Mother Earth with conscious awareness. The human consciousness is evolving. As people wake-up and become aware, we can identify different levels of mindfulness – consciousness. Even a whole new gene-pool is merging.

- **Emerging of a new human gene pool.**

We can identify new human 'sub-species' emerging from *Homo sapiens animalis* to *Homo sapiens sapiens,* to *Homo sapiens individuals* to *Homo sapiens spiritualis.* Below you find our artist's view of this process.

This also denotes the path of Truth. In the process, we will also be tested for what we stand for. We must be clear on what we stand for, because: *'If you stand for nothing, you will fall for everything'.*

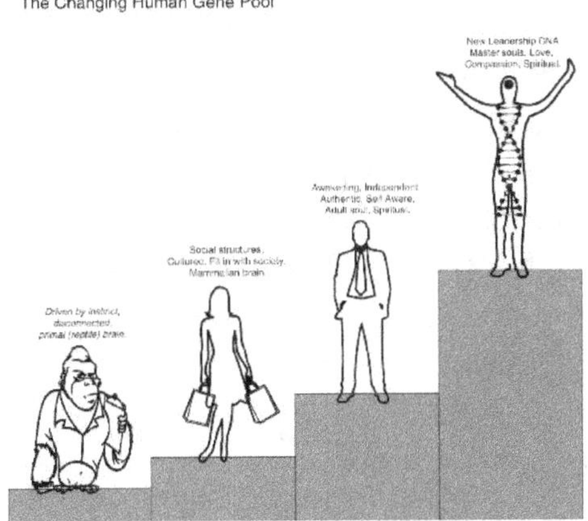

Emerging of a new human gene pool.

In the series, *'Authentic Living and Leading'*, we have outlined how success, prosperity, and happiness are encoded as our original DNA-blueprint. It is suggested that you familiarise yourself with this understanding.[13]

Sabotage by the ego-self.

At the same time, we need to be aware that the shadow ego-self is a hard taskmaster and will not easily give up its hold on the hearts, minds, souls, and lives of those who are now awakening to a new quality of life.

The shadow ego-self aims to maintain the *status quo* and protect the ego-self against any exposure to Truth or Light, as this will be the end of its power-reign. It sabotages all opposition and/or positive contributions and the bearers thereof.

- **Feeding ground of the ego**

The ego needs to feed off emotional dramas and negativity. It also has to keep supporters and relevant feeding/drinking holes in place for survival and self-preservation.

At the same time, the shadow ego-self is frustrated by happy, fulfilled, enlightened people who lead successful lives.

It is this side of our being that needs to be brought to Light and exposed to Truth while we heal the pain, hurt, and ignorance. The authentic self, however, contains all we need to fulfill our purpose and be happy and fulfilled as a blueprint in our multi-dimensional DNA.

- **The inner battle**

An inner battle between the shadow ego-self and the light, real-me, authentic self, is becoming evident and escalating.

These inner dramas are bound to manifest in different forms in our external circumstances and different contexts of human relationships. This includes our relationships, families, friendships, marriages, parenting, partnering, or work-related situations.

- **Breaking free**

The challenge is to break free from the mold or 'bubble' you found yourself in while freeing yourself from outdated mindsets, and values. At the same time you need new power tools and skills to elevate yourself to the next, and a higher level of consciousness.

This includes becoming aware of where you are now and on what level the self, functions.

It also includes understanding where the other person/persons are coming from. It helps to ask the questions: What is my baseline for functioning? What is the 'go-to mode' I operate from?

If it is negative and destructive, now is the time to change. You deserve nothing less than the best. We all do!

One of the greatest challenges we are now facing is to identify authenticity. This includes connecting to and understanding our authentic self while developing our true identity. Our new identity will determine our quality of life.

The question is: What is our 'identity'?

Identity

Identity comes from the word 'idea'. Our identity is all about our ideas about ourselves. It also includes answers to the questions:

- Who do you say you are?
- Where do you get your ideas about yourself?

Our identity refers to what we think about ourselves.

Different people and situations reflect what they think of us. We may internalize these thoughts and make them our own. We, therefore, build our identity or ideas about ourselves, on what other people and the world say about us.

This means we allow the world and other people to determine and define who we think we are. Their ideas become our definition of self and our identity. We can think this is the truth.

Different identities

We have different identities, all depending on where we get our ideas about ourselves from.

This includes an individual, personal, social, and universal spiritual, identity.

We also have different role identities according to the different roles we fulfill.

The most important identity is of course our spiritual identity.

This is a search for Truth, the thoughts of the Creator – God. The road of authenticity is all about the search for truth. This includes the truth about our self, our purpose, and what happiness is.

- **Individual identity**

This refers to persons being conscious of and connected to their authentic self, their inner core, and their unique value as a person.   This includes being aware of your authentic DNA success-blueprint just waiting to be recovered and released. We covered this topic in detail in book 1. 'The authentic self. Who am I? as the first book of the series *Authentic Living and Leading'*.

- **Non-dividable**

The word 'individual' comes from 'non-dividable' and therefore refers to the whole self, healed self, holy self, original or authentic self.

This part of the self is not influenced by the opinion of other people and the changing world. It refers to the continuity of a person over time, although they take on various roles. They may behave differently in different circumstances, but at the core, they stay true to the authentic self.

Now, many people are letting go of their public and social identities to live in honesty and integrity. This is all about getting 'real'.

These people have an integrated, healed, whole, unique individuality, personality, and positive self-image. They know who they are, where they are going, and why. They experience self and life as meaningful.

- **Coping with demands**

Our identity is developed by coping with the demands and problems of life. Our real or authentic self and individual identity will come to the fore, or not when placed under pressure while meeting demands. Whatever your default mode is, will become visible when placed in difficult circumstances.

These trying times can make you bitter or better.

When we choose to live up to our authenticity and truth it also includes accepting our place and responsibility in life in general and in specific situations. Here we find our universal purpose and calling.

However, people with an identity crisis find it difficult to love their real-me individual identity and universal purpose.

- **Overcoming an identity crisis**

People with an identity problem are usually people who cannot solve problems or accept responsibility. They are usually comfortable, lazy, complacent, and choose the easiest escape route.

They lose a part of the self.

This is caused by a radical, fundamental change that results in a person feeling lost, unhinged, disconnected, fearful while experiencing the situation as meaningless. For example, a person officer has a public identity as a police officer with a rank. Suddenly the rank is taken away from him and the public identity disappears. They are ignorant of who they are, beyond the definition of the rank in the police service.

The same occurs when a person is divorced, loses their job, becomes ill or wins the Lotto Jackpot.

These persons then experience an identity crisis. Solutions to an identity crisis can be found in accepting the responsibility to do the inner work and reconnect to the authentic, higher self.

The solution to this dilemma can be found in re-inventing and redefining self by recognizing your identity and asking:

- Who am I? Where do I come from?
- Where am I going? Why?
- What is my purpose?
- How do I become successful and happy?

You will find answers to this question in the book. *'The Authentic self. Who am I?'*

This brings us to the next level of our identity, as our personal identity.

- **Personal identity**

This refers to who other people in your inner personal circle, say you are. These are people close to you. The spouse can see the other person in a different light than their colleagues.

This means you may have different identities at home and work.

When the opinion of other changes, people tend to change their opinion of themselves. Their identity is built on the perceptions of others.

This is a very weak foundation to build your identity on.

Ask yourself.

- Whose opinions do you value most? Why?
- What would happen if their opinion about you changed? Why?

The next level of gaining clarity about our identity is our role identity.

Role identity

We all function in different roles and contexts.

The contextual self or role identity refers to how a person identifies with and accepts responsibility for their roles.

Roles could include being the adult, child, partner, parent, boss, leader, manager, worker, assistant, teacher, preacher, employer, employee, and friend.

- Demands of a role

Each role or context has its demands, rules, responsibilities, boundaries, agreements, and tasks. The role identity develops as a person accepts responsibility for, learns, and lives the rules, skills, and boundaries of a specific role.

New parents can serve as an example. With the arrival of a baby, they are unsure and uninformed. After the third or fourth child, the parental role has developed, and they have more confidence.

It also applies to the career role. It demands knowledge, skills, and time to grow into a new role.

- Want the role - not the responsibility

There are however people who would like the social standing of a role, but don't want the responsibility that goes with the role. People could want the job, but not the work. Someone could want to be a leader or the boss, but not want the responsibilities that accompany the decision-making process.

For example, a man wants a wife for it is socially more acceptable than being single. However, he doesn't want to be a husband and accept the responsibility that comes with being a partner. His priorities still lie with the freedom of being single.

Another example is when parents want children. However, they don't want the responsibility that comes with raising a child. They can get a nanny and/or au pair to do the job for them. Some parents can dump their children with grandparents, a day school, and/or family members. The healthy path is to accept responsibility while employing someone to help when needed – especially when both parents need to work.

- **Flexibility**

Another challenge is the ability to move from one context to another. For example, at work, you are the boss and held in high regard while at home you are a parent and brought down to earth by demanding children, dirty nappies, feeding time, and little rest.

It requires high levels of maturity, awareness, mindfulness, and self-coaching to make the shift from one context to another.

Contextual maturity means that a person can live up to all these demands while managing to juggle all these demands at the same time. The solution is to show up for the game you are playing at that moment. Be present, mindful, and conscious of what role you are fulfilling. Do whatever you need to do to the best of your ability. Remember, nothing lasts forever. Enjoy it while you are there.

• **Public or social identity**

This represents a name and position in society. The public identity develops as a person achieves certain positions. For example, you become the chairperson of a corporation, or a member of the school's governing body, the district surgeon, pastor, butcher, teacher, or any other public role we may occupy.

We can also have a cultural, political, sporting, or financial identity. Like our role identity, each social label comes with a price tag. You are in the social spotlight and under scrutiny.

Here you will need to decide to express your real-me authentic self, or will your ego take over.

The most important identity, however, is our universal identity.

This is where we find the true meaning and purpose of who we are.

- **Universal identity**

The universal identity (aka a spiritual or soul identity) is found within the higher, universal mind – the thoughts of the creator, of God. Here we have a blueprint of who we truly are.

More and more people are awakening and identifying with higher levels of universal consciousness. They are discovering who they are and what the meaning of their life is. People with an identity crisis can find meaning for their lives within the higher mind of Creation – with God.

Our self-esteem[14] will all depend on where we are coming from.

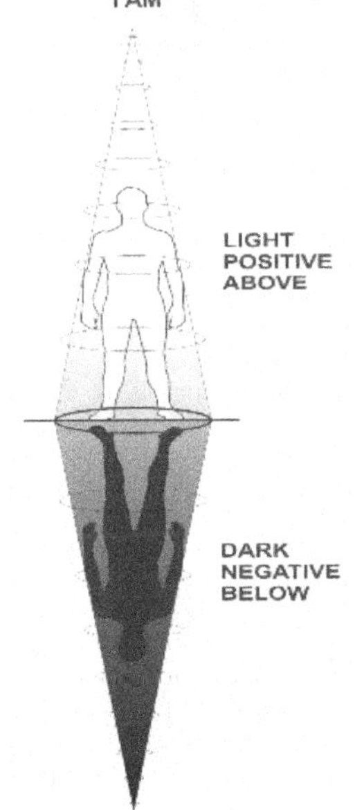

We can come from the authentic, original higher or light self – or the dark, shadow ego-self, as seen in the sketch below.

One of the most important things we need to become conscious of is that our thoughts become things. What we think about- comes about. How we see and think about our self – comes about.

For example, if you think you are unlucky and never win something – you will never win something.

If you believe you deserve to be happy, healthy, wealthy and fulfilled – it will be attracted to you. One side is governed by the ego – the other side by the authentic self – the soul

The quality of your life will all depend on

what side you give authority to. Ask yourself, who makes the defining decisions in my life?

What route you take will all depend on how you think.

Thoughts become things

A thought is an electro-magnetic impulse that causes a stir or wave in the ether. It is transported by the web of life from one point to another. We are, however, not conscious of all this information, as we do not have the highly developed senses, we need to pick up these signals. We are, however, influenced at a deeper subconscious level.

Sometimes it seems as though everything is going right. Plans are working, and a lot of positive progress is made. You lose track of time while enjoying a conversation, listening to inspiring music, or completing a compelling task. The channels are open, we progress with effortless ease, and we feel happy and excited.

Everything is in flow.

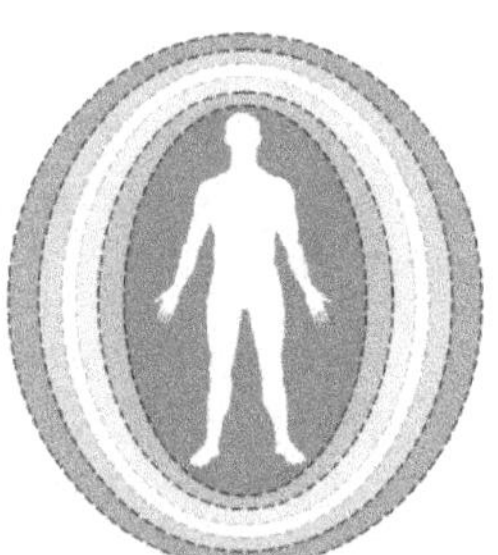 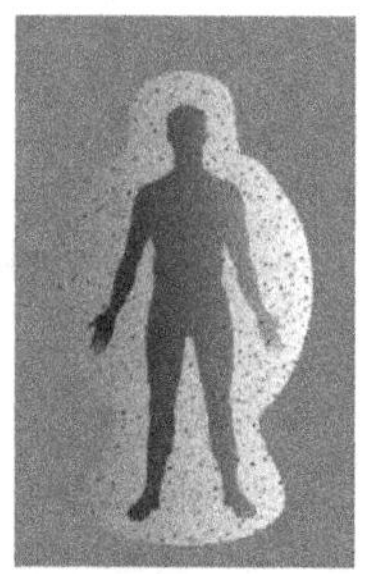

A person open and in flow   **A person blocked**

with negativity

However, sometimes it seems as if everything is going wrong. It doesn't matter what you do, nothing seems to be working the way you would like it to. The truth is that something is blocking the path. A fact is that negativity of any kind inhibits the spin of electrons in their orbit.

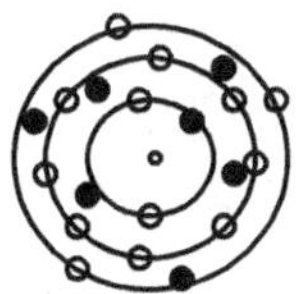

Electron spin impeded by negativity

This lowers the vibrations, causing discord, a false note, or something off-key. If we allow and/or tolerate negativity, we devolve to a lower frequency. At the same time, any negativity creates a blind-spot and we view life through this tainted perception. The negativity we perceive on the outside is a mere reflection of our inner negative programs and dynamics. Resistance doesn't solve the problem, as in essence, we resist our inner fears, hurts, blind-spots, and lack of vision and insight. Whatever we resist – persists.

We can recreate our reality by changing our inner thoughts and programs, as thoughts become things. This means that we first need to clear out our filters.

Filters

The reticular activation system or RAS[15] is a control centre that filters about 100 million pieces of information every second. Our five senses process 20 million pieces of information per second, without us being conscious of the process.

- ## The Reticular Activating System (RAS)

The RAS is the mechanism that filters all this incoming information and alerts us to the tiny fraction of input that is important, and relevant to our goals and plans. Our brain is thus a goal-seeking mechanism. It must have goals! Information will be filtered through according to our plans, goals, wishes, dreams, and visions.

Unfortunately, most of us do not have a clear vision of what we want, nor do we have precise written goals and plans. The RAS then has to use the second-best information available, namely the messages and goals from our dominant thoughts.

This default setting can be or from the shadow ego-self, or the real-me authentic self. You need to choose what side of self will determine the direction of your life.

These default goals allow the RAS to effectively sift through the 100 million pieces of information coming into our brain at a deeper level of consciousness. By writing and visualizing our goals, we replace the default goals with new, precise goals, and powerful successful outcomes.

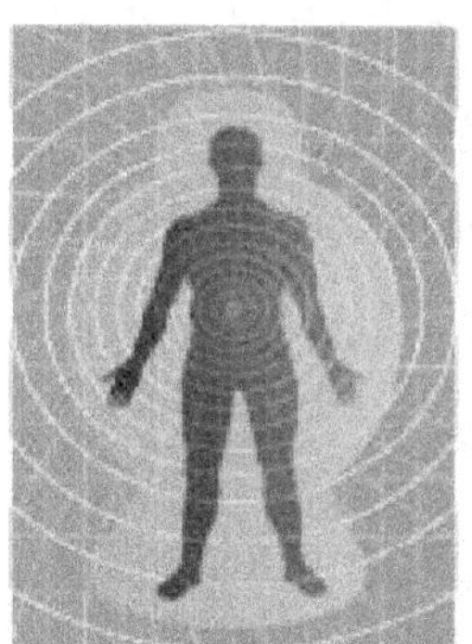

The RAS or our filter system

When you identify positive end-results, they are locked into the RAS that works like a magnet, attracting to you whatever your default thoughts may be. What you think about starts to come about and – thoughts become things.

- **The power of a plan**

Various studies have shown that less than 5 percent of people have a written plan of how they intend to obtain their goals or how to create the future they want and desire.

When we focus on our fears, limitations, and what we don't want to happen, and do not have positive goals, our fears become the prominent default goals in our RAS.

We then begin to experience and attract the things we don't want! We experience failure, loss, limitations, worry, and anxiety. This reinforces our erroneous perceptions and processing of information. This becomes a vicious circle that could last a whole lifetime. All we need to do is wake up, become conscious, and get connected and switched on — for a quality life and living.

Power positions

The switch of the RAS 'power station' has two positions—on/high or off/low. When the switch is on 'on/high', a lot of brain energy is generated that stimulates high internal energy flow and activities.

- **Connected – 'on'**

A person who is connected, centred, and grounded is also a person who is 'switched on'. They are fully conscious of the self and life. This person can produce their own inner motivation, focus, and regulate their energy levels. Because of the high inner activity, it can manifest in external activity and actions that take them forward.

These people can think for themselves and do things on their own. They live from the deepest core to the outside and are constantly busy developing their own unique potential.

They have vision, goals, and desires, and are focused on a quality life and serving people. Each problem or crisis is seen as an opportunity for growth and development. They are 'switched on' for successful living.

- **Disconnected – 'off'**

On the other hand, when the energy switch is on 'off/low', there is minimal internal action. People then rely on external stimulation and find it difficult to function without the motivation and stimulation of other people and situations.

This is the setting of the shadow ego-self that feeds off the energy from others.

This is found in every life situation. Children think their parents and teachers should care for them, stimulate them, and think on their behalf. Spouses think their partners should make them happy and think on their behalf, and churchgoers think that their religious leaders should guide them.

- **Abdicating personal responsibility**

In these practices, people believe that there is something or someone in a 'higher position' of power than themselves, who will accept responsibility for the quality of their lives and make them happy. There is little indication of personal responsibility, development of potential, and making a personal contribution to life. They have no vision or goals, and their desires are unclear and are mostly negative, and they see each problem as a stumbling block. These people are switched 'off'.

In reality, nothing out of the ordinary happens. They count on external stimulation, practices, and appearances, to make them happy. This usually does not happen. Should the external stimulation and practices disintegrate, they return to their switched-off state. Life once again looks bleak, meaningless, and without purpose.

- **Blaming and shaming**

Some people can remain in this switched-off situation and believe that this is the way life is – forever. Sometimes this state can be bridged in the search for external stimulation, pleasure, and practices that provide temporary relief.

Shadow ego-dwellers are never really happy and fulfilled. They usually have health, relationship, and/or financial problems as well. They usually think that life is giving them a raw deal.

They look for answers outside themselves, and blame others for their difficult lives, while they see themselves as victims. They also shame, label, ostracize, belittle, and/or condemn any opposition and resistance. The reason is the fear of being exposed and the inability to cope. They are also fearful of change and the unknown.

As said, the ego is a hard taskmaster and will not readily let go of its power over your decision-making process, and your life.

- **Energy vampires**

Shadow ego-dwellers are not only disconnected from themselves and life but live off or through others. It is very energy draining to continuously support passive people and to motivate, activate, and provide them with energy.

These people are energy thieves or vampires. They can actively or passively seek attention and energy from others and become active or passive manipulators or intimidators. Others are just as effective in this by being aloof, by giving the silent treatment, or trying the 'poor me' act.

These destructive power games need to be identified and stopped. Should some people not want to leave their comfort zones and stay dependent on others, they will soon realize that they are going to be left behind and alone in the desert of life.[16]

This is a very stressful situation to be in. However, there is a solution. We can move to a different level of functioning.

Different levels of functioning

There are different levels of functioning.

Some levels are positive and productive, while others are less positive and productive, even negative and destructive.

• Triggering powerful brain-rhythms

When everything seems to be going right and all worries and anxieties are removed, you have triggered the slower brain rhythms. Slower brain rhythms enable us to create the life and world we would like to have. This is where our answers, solutions, and vision of the future can be found.

The importance of a deeper understanding, knowledge, training, and implementation of slower more powerful brain rhythms, inner peace, and tranquillity will gain momentum in the new era. We will address these power-settings in book 6 *'Power Intelligence. The intelligence of the future'[17]*, in the series *'Authentic Living and Leading'*.

UNCONSCIOUS		CONSCIOUS		
Delta	**Theta**	**Alpha**	**Beta**	**Gamma**
0.5–4 Hz	4–8 Hz	8–13 Hz	13–30 Hz	30–42 Hz
Instinct	Emotion	Consciousness	Thought	Will
Deep sleep Trance or Nonphysical state Coma/ unconscious	Drives Feelings Dreams Trance Integration of feelings	Relaxation Meditation Focus Body awareness Super learning	Perception Concentration Mental activity Alertness Arousal	Extreme focus, Energy Ecstasy

Above you find a summary of these levels of consciousness.[18]

• The importance of understanding

The importance of understanding and implementing, not only right- and left-brain functioning, but implementing different levels of functioning, cannot be underestimated. The knowledge, skills, and understanding will enable us to create the world, life, peace, happiness, and prosperity, we owe to ourselves and others.

Our challenge is to know where we are coming from and what our approach to the self and life is. There are only one of two possibilities: We either come from our shadow ego-self – or our enlightened authentic self.

Ego-centered versus soul-centered living

The summary on the next page indicates one of the two paths we could follow. [19]

What you should know and how to activate it', you will find all the necessary tools and skills to change your life to the resonance of love, light, power, wisdom, and abundance. When we look at all our masters from all religions, we find that they totally identified with their higher soul-self - even their Monad. They became one with their inner light authentic self, or personal Christ self, or enlightened self.

SOUL-CENTRED	EGO-CENTRED
Self-aware	Self-conscious
Self-worth	Self-centred
Self-esteem	Self-importance
Self-care	Self-serving
Self-confidence	Self-delusion
Self-respect	Self-indulgence
Self-mastery	Self-destructive

Soul-centred versus ego-centred living

The word 'Christ' comes from the Latin word *Christos* meaning 'the anointed of God' – the anointed with Light/Love.

Our challenge is to become light-bearers. Our challenge is to become anointed with light. However, first, we need to choose between the two paths of life.

Above you find a summary of the soul-centred and ego-centred approaches to life. For more information see New Success DNA and New Leadership DNA.

Outline of Daily Power Tools for Power People

We have identified 52 power tools we all need to master. Each week of the year covers a specific topic. A topic is divided into seven different aspects that are covered over each day of that specific week.

You can mindfully turn every new understanding into a power tool you can use to coach yourself to ultimate success. Ultimate success means having access to everything you want and need at the time you need it. It is not about stockpiling and hoarding. See book 2 '*The Authentic Self. Coaching yourself to ultimate success,* in the series *'Authentic living and Leading'*, for more information

Over 365 days – you will develop all the skills and tools you need to coach yourself to a happy, fulfilling life.

Not only will this empower you personally, but it will empower and inspire those around you as well. Together we will synergize this new energy and begin to create a new momentum of happiness, resilience, wellness, and quality living, that benefits all people.

Guidelines for using this book

We first have to pay attention to time and timing.

• Time

We have different kinds of time scales or 'calendars'. We find *Chronos* or chronological time according to our traditional solar-lunar (sun and moon cycles) system, where processes unfold in chronological order.

There are 52 weeks with 7 days each. This gives us 365 days in our solar-lunar year. An extra day is added for a leap year that comes around every four years.

• Kairos time

We also have *Kairos* time that refers to a larger cosmic time scale or the time of the Creator.

According to ancient timescales the cosmic seasons of 36 000 years and 360 000 solar-lunar years, finished off on 21 December 2012. At the same time, we need to remember that our inner 'biological clocks' and also our 'clock genes' are set according to universal time scales, or *kairos* time. Our biological clock and general cycles are set according to our solar-lunar systems.

It is important to remember that our multi-dimensional potential, including our spiritual DNA, chromosomes, and genes, are all aligned and synchronized with *Chronos* and *Kairos* time.

• Aligning with Kairos time

The cosmic *Kairos* time scale includes and encompasses our smaller solar-lunar *Chronos* system.

It is now *Kairos* time.

We can expect that our disabled junk genes and clock genes will from now on become enabled and activated. We can also take control and consciously activate these processes to create more flow, happiness, and success in our lives.

It is time!

By being mindful of these processes, we can consciously align ourselves and synchronize our potential with *kairos* time, while still taking our *Chronos* solar-lunar time scale, into consideration.

For convenience, we start on the first day of every year.

Weekly topics

Each week starts with a specific topic, for example, in week one our topic is happiness. Every day you will find an aspect of that topic and the meaning it has in your life.

The shadow side is also outlined so that you can become aware of and identify it in yourself and/or others when it rears its ugly head.

On the next page you find an example of your daily power tools.

This includes:

- The topic of the week
- The power tool for that day
- The approach of the authentic self
- The approach of the shadow ego-self
- Holding the power for the day
- Redefining self
- Setting goals for the day

There are also some suggestions and power tools to help you coach yourself and master the situations of life with more confidence.

Set your goals to practice specific skills every day. In that way, you will develop more power tools and experience how your power escalates.

Spend this new-found power wisely and with confidence.

DAILY POWER TOOLS FOR A POWER PERSON

WEEK 52: LOVE

Who makes the decisions in your life?

DAY 365: ARRIVAL

We have arrived at the end of this year. Over the last year, we have learned to clean up the disarray and complete all unfinished tasks and business in our lives. Now we have arrived. This arrival marks the end of an old path and the start of a new journey. Arrival and departure are therefore at exactly the same place. allow your authentic self to take control of your new year.

THE SHADOW SIDE

There is no place in a cluttered life of the shadow ego-self that is full of the debris of past failures, unfinished business, anger, resentment, and incomplete tasks, for something new. This means that the fragmented shadow self is constantly on the road without a destination or a point of arrival – in short- shadow ego-dwellers are lost!

FOR TODAY

Make sure that you have cleaned out all your physical clutter and cleared up all your emotional, mental, religious, and even financial and family baggage. Mark your point of arrival and celebrate. You now know you can embark on a new journey with a clear conscience in the new year. You can now relax and celebrate this exciting time in your life. On the first day of the new year, we depart once again.

TODAY WE HOLD IN OUR AWARENESS: The power of **Arrival**

TODAY I AM: Arriving/Home

MY GOALS FOR TODAY ARE:

....

....

From the book: Power Tools for Power People

A specific thought or power tool for every day has been included. The reason is that the more people who share a specific thought, the more powerful it becomes. You can imagine the power that will be generated when we all share the same thought every day of the year.

Just start

Do not worry if you don't start at week one, day one. Join in and start where we all are at that specific time and place. If you are not sure, look it up on the website. Remind yourself daily that you are also part of the universal mind and that you too – like everyone else – are bringing your unique self as a piece of the puzzle to the table of life. Together we can and will change the fabric of life into a tapestry and kaleidoscope of color and brilliance. We will do it day by day, step by step, and thought by thought. Remember that every great victory was achieved by thousands of smaller feats.

Steps in using this book

It is recommended that you follow the steps below before you go to sleep at night. The reason is that the subconscious mind and soul never sleep. It will immediately begin processing the new information while saving it in your long-term memory during the night. In this way, you will be prepared for the new day when you wake up in the morning in ways beyond your wildest imagination. This is why we 'sleep on it'.

Step 1: Every evening, read the topic for the next day. For example, if you want to start on 1 January, you need to read the relevant section on the evening of 31 December to prepare for 1 January. On the evening of 1 January you prepare for 2 January, and so forth.

Step 2: Remind yourself of the topic for that week and the power tool for the next day.

Step 3: Read through the light side description of the power tool and get a clear picture in your mind of what you need to expect from your authentic light self the next day.

Step 4: Read through the negative shadow side to be mindful if, when, and how it rears its ugly head during the coming day/days.

Step 5: Read through the power tools you can implement to master yourself and any negative situation that may arise during the next day/days.

Step 6: Make a shortlist of these tools and set them as personal goals for the next day, for example, I must remember to stay grounded. Commit yourself to your personal goals.

Step 7: Confirm your new identity and the thought of the day by repeating: I AM (grounded) (loving) (happy) .... etc. In this way, you make it your point of view. You become what you believe in. You will also know what to stand for in the future.

Step 8: Make the thought of the day the last thing in your mind before you fall asleep.

Remember, this is how we place the topic for the following day in our higher mind. This will also automatically be triggered when you need it the most.

Step 9: When you wake up in the morning before you open your eyes, remind yourself of the thought of the day. Recap the power tool and remind yourself of your goal/s for the day. The moment you put your feet on the ground say, Today I AM (loving) (happy) (grounded) or whatever the power tool for the day is. Confirm this with your feet on the ground.

Step 10: Stay mindful of the fact that all over the globe people are sharing your mindset. Remind yourself that we are all connected.

Step 11: Go about your daily life as usual. Remember that the higher mind never sleeps and will assist and remind you by making you aware of what to do, say and act, and how to handle the little nitty-gritty things and people in life.

You can use this book over and over every year while you recap all your power skills and tools. They are relevant for anyone and everyone who has a dream, wish, desire, and intention to be happy and fulfilled and lead a quality life.

As these are fundamental universal principles – we find them in every nation, culture, creed, and religion that is committed to the advancement of humanity into a positive future where all will be able to live quality lives. This means these power tools can and will never become outdated.

Setting goals and intentions

When you embark on this path of empowering yourself, you also need to know where to channel this new energy. You need a new focus and vision. You obtain your vision or dream by setting goals and stating your intentions.

- **Vision**

A vision is a picture in your mind of what you and your life could be in the future. To make it easier and clearer for yourself, draw a lifeline (such as the one below) and mark it in ten-year intervals with each year clearly denoted.

Start at the end of your life (+/- 80 years is about the average lifespan). Ask yourself: What do I want in my life at this stage? The general answers are things like a home that is paid for; a loving partner, good health, a family that is happy and fulfilled with children, grandchildren, and maybe even great-grandchildren; physical and mental health; financial independence, friends, etc.

---10-------20 --------30-------40--------50-------60-------70-------80--

Your lifeline

However, very few people realize that to get to this level, they need to start earlier in life. Mark how old you are now and summarise what you have, want, and need.

Write down your wants, needs, wishes, dreams, and desires. Be clear on who you are and what makes you happy.

The Divine Universe will work with you on this plan for your life and support every effort according to your unique blueprint program you already have within your DNA.

• Dreams, desires, and intentions

However, if you do not have a plan and are without a personal vision and/or dreams, clear goals, and intentions, the universe will work with your default program. If not clarified, this could be the dark, destructive force from your shadow ego-self. You will be mindlessly creating more of what you *do not want*.

So – take back your power and reclaim your life from the lower ego-self. Stop struggling with what you don't want. Be clear about what you do want. Identify what makes you really happy. Set clear intentions

• Know where you are coming from

It is important to know where you are coming from. If you are not sure, you can find out by doing your PI Success Profile (PISP) that will be available in 2021.

• Be aware of your wellbeing

Your spiritual and emotional wellness is just as important as your physical wellbeing. You attract into your proximity everything that resonates on your frequency. If you want something new, change your resonance. This is the law of attraction. To do this you need new tools and skills. This is what this book is all about.

If you come from the lower, shadow ego-self you might not obtain all these things. Your health will deteriorate under the pressure of negativity and the rest of your life will be self-destructive. You will be sitting and waiting for death to relieve you from this earthly struggle and suffering.

However, if you come from the authentic self, you will find great fulfillment at a mature age. All your dreams, visions, and intentions will be fulfilled and all your goals will be accomplished.

You will also have the knowledge and wisdom that, while you are still here you still have a purpose to fulfill. Here you find purpose, meaning, adventure, and excitement as part of everyday life. You will only die and move on when your task has been fulfilled. You will be happy and fulfilled and ready to let go of your earthly existence.

However, to get to this place you will need to plan and set goals and put out your intentions that could be physical, spiritual, and/or mystical. Don't sell yourself short.

Remember – you can have it all!

Setting goals

Goal setting is primarily a mental exercise. Take your lifeline and identify what needs to be done within the next ten, five, and one year.

Formulate your goals and identify the actions needed to achieve these goals. The brain and our mental wiring are all goal orientated. We always have to work or move towards something to maintain flow and keep the juices flowing.

The five steps of goal setting

1. Have a vision of what you want to achieve.

2. What must you do to achieve this? Always identify your plan A, plan B, and Plan C. Understand that plan A doesn't necessarily always work.

3. Assessment: If plan A doesn't work, you need a different method. Assess the situation and make changes as needed. You also need a method of assessment to determine your progress in the process. You can do your Power Intelligence Success Profile (PISP) on the internet (http://www.powerintelligence.net) to help you.

4. Be flexible, change, grow, and assess your progress. Read the books New *Success DNA: What you should know and how to activate it* and Power *Intelligence: Mastering your miracle mind.* (E-books are available on http://www.brendahattinghshop.co.za)

5. Celebrate, celebrate, celebrate!!

- **Setting intentions**

Where goal setting is a mental exercise, intentions are a soul and spiritual exercise. Intentions are exactly what the word says: you are 'in-tension' between something and someone on the one hand, and something else or someone else on the other hand. This is the clear-cut difference between the lower shadow ego-self and the higher light authentic self.

These parts of self want different things at the same time. The reason is that they come from different perspectives and value systems. They have directly opposing perspectives.

By consciously connecting to your higher authentic self and setting your intentions from your heart, mind soul, and spirit, you also align your intentions with the flow and will of the Divine Universe. Here you will find all the love, support, understanding, and also resources to make your dreams, visions, intentions, and desires come true.

Success is not about what you are acquiring and accomplishing. Success is all about who you are becoming in the process. You let go of the outcome and allow the processes to unfold in a divine way and method. In the process, you become who you were supposed to be – the authentic quality you!

Genuine authentic intentions come from your heart and soul. This is also the dream, wish, and soul purpose you have in your heart and feel in your gut. This is also the dream, wish, vision, and desires the divine Universe has for you. These are the thoughts of God.

Einstein said:

'I only want to know the thoughts of God – the rest is minor detail'.

When setting your intentions, become still, go into your silent place within and find out what the higher authentic self and your soul have installed for you. They are the messengers of your Creator. Stay here and listen to your inner voice, heart, and higher mind and receive your guidance. Now, go and set your intentions as directed. Set your goals and identify what you should do.

Remember that miracles are also encoded into your blueprint. So expect miracles to happen as part of a natural everyday occurrence. Be grateful – and celebrate!

- **Your daily power tool**

Use your daily power tool to co-create what you want and need. You can get your daily power tool by visiting us on Twitter at the address: www.twitter.com/drBrendaInc This will help you to synergize with everyone else who is also on the 'same page'.

Suggestions

When we grow in our awareness, we also begin to understand spiritual laws and how the divine universe functions. Connecting to our universal force and creating and maintaining flow – is the ultimate form of success.

This includes becoming aware of the timing, harmony, balance, and rhythm of everything. Any imbalance, disconnection, negativity, or discord we allow, creates resistance, friction, and struggle.

We can stop this destructive process by using our power tools. This includes:

- Detoxifying your body, mind, soul, and spirit
- Cleaning out all the clutter in your life
- Disconnecting from negativity.

You are then open and free to align yourself with your universal power and harness this natural process of flow and success.

You can also consciously choose to align yourself with the flow of universal processes by using these skills and power tools.

Extra power tools

The suggestion is to include the following 'extras' with every power tool you learn each day. These 'extras' below can power-boost your life, business, relationship, and fast-forward intentions, plans, visions, and desires.

It will cost you some extra time and effort to make use of those 'extra power tools' by creating a daily or weekly mantra, affirmation, symbol, prayer, or banner. Here are a few suggestions you can keep in mind to enhance your progress.

- ### **Mantras and affirmations**

An affirmation is something that we pronounce and confirm as true.

We make an affirmative statement of something we support, like: '*I love you*'.

This truth can be affirmed in various verbal and non-verbal ways that include writing poetry, making up rhymes, or singing songs and mantras. You can write a song or poem about love, honesty, happiness, fun, or integrity. You can also create a mantra.

A mantra is a rhythmic song or tune. The rhythm and rhyme of a verse create synergy with the greater universal rhythms, and you can feel the pulse of life flowing through you as you sing or recite your mantra. Mantras are in essence poems that you can also sing. Here are a few examples of mantras:

> '*I am at peace, I am at rest - I receive only the best.*'

A very powerful mantra is:

> '*I am a being of violet fire – I am the purity God desires.*'

You can also use this for others and substitute 'I' for anybody else. Your mantra will then go like this:

> '*Bobby* (or any other name) *is a being of violet fire –*
>
> *Bobby* (or any other name), *is the purity* (health, happiness, success, or any other wish you have for this person) *God desires.*

Another example is:

> *I am healthy, wealthy, and happy –*
> *All good things come to me*"

There are many books with more mantras. You can also find mantras on the internet. Mantras can also be used as prayers or prayers as mantras.

- **Prayers**

Prayers can include a request, wish, hope, or plea that is spoken or done silently. Masters like Jesus Christ left us a powerful prayer in the reciting of the *Our Father.* Likewise, repeating the *'Hail Mary'* is also very powerful.

Prayers and mantras can be personal or impersonal; formal or informal. There are many books on poetry, prayers, and mantras available.

Follow your heart.

- **Affirmations, declarations, and fiats.**

A declaration is an announcement, affirmation, or statement you make about something or someone. Fiat is an arbitrary order or decree – like: *'I swear it is hot today!'* in essence this is an oath. Other fiats include 'promises' and 'giving your word'.

The 'word' is a very powerful tool, and we need to 'count our words' because each word will come back to you for a reckoning. A decree is a kind of prayer in the form of a declaration, order, law, ruling, or verdict and is very powerful. The most powerful decree we find is the decree:

'Let there be light!'

When you know who you are, you also are aware of your purpose, position, and power on earth. You can choose to identify with the power given to you – or not. We are custodians of this planet and we were created to take dominion over this physical reality. To 'take dominion' means you know who you are, what your power is and you choose to use it according to the universal laws – the law of God. You take dominion over adversity and physicality by accepting your place as co-creator with the Divine. You become the living law – the living Truth. You become the living Word like the master, Jesus Christ.

Examples of decrees are:

'I decree the end of struggle'

'Let there be the flow of abundance now.'

'Let there be healing and happiness for Bobby (or any other name)'

Once again you can change the names of people and desires you have for them and yourself. Remember a decree is a law – so keep it synchronized and synergized with the universal laws and truth that is – unconditional love and compassion for all.

This becomes more significant if you can put up a sign or signal marking your decree. For example. a person declares/decrees a new building or bridge is open and cuts the ribbon as a symbol that it is now in use. This symbolizes the end of something and the beginning of a new chapter. The decree becomes your law.

Be careful to use decrees without a deep soul search, cleansing, and clarity concerning your motives and intentions. This is not something to be taken lightly.

- **Markers and symbols**

Put up markers or use symbols to remind you of important choices and changes you made. Make a mark on the ground where you experience something significant. You can do this silently without anyone knowing.

On the other hand, you can do something very special to mark the occasion. The Taj Mahal was built in India by Shah Jahan for his wife to mark their love and her passing on. You don't need to be this extravagant. You do however need to be sincere, real, authentic, and truthful – with yourself.

- **Create a banner**

A banner is a poster, sign, placard, or flag you can use to remind yourself of something important. Where developing your power tools is concerned, you can make a 'weekly banner' for each theme.

For example:

Banner for week 9: Fun:

I am finding the funny and the funny is finding me

Banner for week 12: Truth

'Truth sets you free'

Banner for Week 29: Honesty

'Honesty is the best policy'

- **Be creative.**

Be creative with the reprogramming of your heart and mind. Sing, paint, dance, or make music. Recite your mantras frequently. Pray earnestly. Consciously make your decrees and be mindful about your banner for the day or week. Remind yourself and others of the true power we all have within.

Be creative and put your banner for the week (or day/month/year) on a card and paste it where you can see it frequently during the day. This can also be used for a family household where you place the banner for the week on the fridge or where everyone can see it. It is also useful in the office where you paste it close to the coffee or water stations or where everyone can see it.

On a subconscious level, this reminds people of who they are and where the true power in life can be found.

Your power Tools.

On the pages below you find a summary of the power tools we will cover over one year.

The power tools for the first week have been included to get your started.

You can access the rest on the website: www.brendhattingh.com

It's all free.

Remember

- The new energy that you are now going to release by implementing these power tools also needs a new and positive outlet. So get active – jog, go to the gym, take a walk, play with the kids, play golf or tennis, or do any other positive physical activity. It is no use releasing all this new energy if you do not channel it to benefit yourself and those around you.

- You can use the same steps for your family, office, team, or group of friends. Remember that all over the world others are also sharing exactly the same process and the same thoughts.

All over the globe, someone is going to bed, and someone is getting up and starting a new day while holding these thoughts for you.

Return the favor and ... have fun!

Stay connected – stay safe.

Brenda Hattingh

ooo0ooo

DAILY POWER TOOLS

WEEK 1: HAPPINESS

WEEK 2: FREEDOM

WEEK 3: LOVE

WEEK 4: PASSION

WEEK 5: INSPIRATION

WEEK 6: BEAUTY

WEEK 7: PEACE

WEEK 8: GRATITUDE

WEEK 9: FUN

WEEK 10: COMPASSION

WEEK 11: HONOUR

WEEK 12: TRUTH

WEEK 13: INTEGRITY

WEEK 14: FAITHFULNESS

WEEK 15: HUMOUR

WEEK 16: GENTLENESS

WEEK 17: MASTERY

WEEK 18: VICTORY

WEEK 19: ADVENTURE

WEEK 20: CONTENTMENT

WEEK 21: EXPECTATIONS

WEEK 22: COOPERATION

WEEK 23: KINDNESS

WEEK 24: PLEASURE

WEEK 25: SERENITY

WEEK 26: ACCEPTANCE

WEEK 27: FREEDOM

WEEK 28: FORGIVENESS

WEEK 29: HONESTY

WEEK 30: COMMUNICATION

WEEK 31: FAITH

WEEK 32: SELF-CONTROL

WEEK 33: WELLBEING

WEEK 34: ANTICIPATION

WEEK 35: HEALING

WEEK 36: DETACHMENT

WEEK 37: SUPPORT

WEEK 38: ELATION

WEEK 39: MAKING AMENDS

WEEK 40: DESERVING

WEEK 41: VICTORIOUS

WEEK 42: BRILLIANCE

WEEK 43: PURPOSE

WEEK 44: EXCELLENCE

WEEK 45: FULFILMENT

WEEK 46: PRIDE

WEEK 47: LIBERTY

WEEK 48: ATONEMENT

WEEK 49: DEATH

WEEK 50: BIRTH

WEEK 51: NEW DAWN

WEEK 52: LOVE

WEEK 1: HAPPINESS

Happiness is a very elusive concept and very few people really know what it means. However, everyone is looking for 'happiness' or, more correctly, their concept of 'happiness'. This means most people are lost and running around in circles while chasing after a self-made illusion of 'happiness'. Sometimes they never find it and remain lost and running around in circles. Nothing happens until something stops them and brings them to the truth/Truth.

The truth about happiness is that you can never find it because happiness is not lost. It is you and I who are/were lost. We lose our happiness connection when we get too involved in the negativities of life and all it demands. Mostly, we were never connected to the 'happiness resonance' in the first place because our parents, family, friends, society, education system, and/or religion were/are also disconnected, to begin with, so we took/take on their values, skills, and tools. This, however, does not work and never will. Happiness can only be experienced. This means that we lost the connection to and experience of happiness. The solution is that we can consciously reconnect and once again experience happiness!

Happiness is the result of being connected to the higher frequencies of the universe, source, light-love, or any name you would like to use to describe the Deity. In short – God.

We experience flow and freedom when we consciously choose to connect to love and cosmic light – to God. This can take us into still higher dimensions of happiness, rapture, ecstasy, and bliss. While the shadow dweller looks for these experiences in drugs and other illusionary methods, we can claim what is rightfully ours and experience this every day just by being conscious of this universal gift of happiness in all its forms.

Take back your power this week and reconnect to happiness and all it has to offer.

WEEK 1: HAPPINESS

DAY 1: LIGHT-LOVE

THE LIGHT SIDE

Cosmic light or light-love is the essence of reality that forms the foundation and backdrop to our physical reality. Everything physical has its origins in cosmic light/spirit/love or God. It is the Truth that permeates everything and everyone. Light-love binds and keeps everything and everyone together – whole and holy.

THE SHADOW SIDE

Shadow dwellers are unaware, mindless, or not conscious of our basic essence of light-love. The shadow ego-self develops different dark and depressing mechanisms to survive. This illusionary ego-self is driven by self-preservation, fear, and anxiety.

FOR TODAY

Stay conscious of the two polarities and what they stand for. Remember there is only cosmic light that is love-light, Source, God, or any name you would like to choose. The rest is an absence of light that in essence is an illusion. Be mindful of the ego-self living the illusion and the authentic self living Truth. Herein lies your first step to happiness.

TODAY WE HOLD IN OUR AWARENESS: The power of **Divine Love**

TODAY I AM: Light. Love

MY GOALS FOR TODAY ARE:

WEEK 1: HAPPINESS

DAY 2: FLOW

THE LIGHT SIDE

This is the ability to keep the light-love flowing in all circumstances. The whole universe is in constant ebb and flow as it is the pulse of life. Chaos and order are two polarities of the same universal rhythmic process.

THE SHADOW SIDE

All negativity, fears, lies, and untruths block the flow of light-love. These blockages cause disease, decay, and destruction. All disease is just a physical manifestation of the blockage of flow. The answer lies in opening the system and allowing in more love and cosmic light.

FOR TODAY

Stay aware of negative people, what they stand for and how they can influence your life. Create flow by opening yourself to more love and light.

TODAY WE HOLD IN OUR AWARENESS: The power of **Flow**

TODAY I AM: In flow

MY GOALS FOR TODAY ARE:

....

....

WEEK 1: HAPPINESS

DAY 3: FREEDOM

THE REAL-ME AUTHENTIC SELF

We were created to be free – it is encoded into our DNA. The problem arose when we became disconnected and 'fell from grace'; when we lost our innocence. However, on the journey back we are enabling our connections and regaining our inherent wisdom.

THE SHADOW SIDE

Shadow ego-dwellers create a delusional life of the lie. This alternative universe protects the ego. The ego cannot let go of this alternative reality for its mere existence depends on maintaining the delusion. It makes you believe it is real.

FOR TODAY

Identify and assess your fears and the fears of others. Know that this is an illusion.

TODAY WE HOLD IN OUR AWARENESS: The power of **Freedom**

TODAY I AM: Free

MY GOALS FOR TODAY ARE:

....
....
....
....

.WEEK 1: HAPPINESS

DAY 4: ELATION

THE REAL-ME AUTHENTIC SELF

We find various degrees of happiness that vary from mild satisfaction to happiness, bliss, elation, ecstasy, and rapture. Higher levels like ecstasy and rapture come from an extreme release of energy. Here we experience the highest level of freedom, pleasure, happiness, and fulfilment. Only the authentic self can access these levels. Unfortunately, the body cannot maintain this energy for long and we then return to happiness once more.

THE SHADOW SIDE

The shadow ego-self has depression as a default setting. It needs to artificially stimulate feelings of happiness, elation, and ecstasy - usually with stimulants and/or drugs.

FOR TODAY

Stay aware of how people choose to live life in agony or ecstasy. Choose to connect to the higher forms of happiness like elation, ecstasy, and rapture. See how long you can hold this energy/vibe. Try to feel this energy - even if it is just for a moment. See how long you can maintain this experience before you return to lower frequencies or even octaves. Practice...

TODAY WE HOLD IN OUR AWARENESS: The **Power of Elation**

TODAY I AM: Elated

MY GOALS FOR TODAY ARE:

WEEK 1: HAPPINESS

DAY 5: ECSTASY

THE REAL-ME AUTHENTIC SELF

We experience ecstasy when we experience moments of authentic love. Ecstasy is the result of the flow of every/cosmic light through our body, mind, soul, and spirit. This brings freedom and the experience of the highest level of joy, happiness, fulfilment, and delight. This is a rare experience. You can however train your heart and mind to become accustomed to this high level of power by loving yourself.

THE SHADOW SIDE

Some people may never, ever experience the highest levels of happiness, joy, and ecstasy. The reason is that their go-to place is negativity and depression. This could be a permanent setting for those who are disconnected from love and light. Artificial replacements only lead to further destruction.

FOR TODAY

Become still. Generate the feeling of ecstasy within yourself. Feel it in your heart, mind soul, and spirit. See how long you can maintain this level of awareness and power. This will free you from negativity, depression, addictive behavior. Practice regularly.

TODAY WE HOLD IN OUR AWARENESS: The power of **Ecstasy**

TODAY I AM: In ecstasy

MY GOALS FOR TODAY ARE:

WEEK 1: HAPPINESS

DAY 6: JOY

THE REAL-ME AUTHENTIC SELF

Joy is a state of heart and mind. It is the inner experience of being safe and feeling fulfilled and happy. This is the go-to place of the authentic self. You can make joy your go-to place for your life.

THE SHADOW SIDE

When ego-driven people are caught up in miserable situations, they revert further into anger, depression, and despair. They lose their passion for life and living and have nothing to look forward to. They could then turn outward and seek happiness and joy from others or indulge in the illusion of happiness that the shadow world offers.

FOR TODAY

Be still and feel the joy bubble up from within when you connect to love compassion and your authentic being. Create moments of joy and bliss for yourself. Don't rely on others to do this for you. Be mindful of the power of music, fragrances, light, and touch to soothe your mind and heal your soul. Confirm your emotional baseline as joy. Live a joyous life of love and compassion.

TODAY WE HOLD IN OUR AWARENESS: The power of real, from the heart JOY.

TODAY I AM: JOYFUL

MY GOALS FOR TODAY ARE:...........................

WEEK 1: HAPPINESS

DAY 7: HEAVEN

THE REAL-ME AUTHENTIC SELF

Every belief system has a vision of the ultimate place of fulfilment, happiness, joy, ecstasy, aND rapture. It is known by many names, such as Nirvana, New Earth, or New Jerusalem, or heaven. It is our true home as this is where the authentic self, dwells. This place is within; a place from where we can 'download' whatever we need or desire. So above – so below. So within – so without.

THE SHADOW SIDE

Disconnection from and experiencing the illusion or the absence of love-light is 'hell'. The ego dwells here in a self-made lie to create the illusion of home. This is delusional and no money, luxury, position, and/or possessions can make it real and authentic.

FOR TODAY

Know that you can choose 'heaven' or 'hell' experiences every moment of the day. It all depends on what you focus on. Heaven is in essence a safe haven where you experience, health, wealth, happiness, and success. It is not necessarily a place - it is rather a vibe, a resonance, a level of consciousness, and mindfulness. Get connected. Calibrate your baseline to the 'heaven/haven' setting. Be prepared for wonderful surprises. Be amazed.

TODAY WE HOLD IN OUR AWARENESS: The power of **Heaven**

TODAY I AM: In Heaven

MY GOALS FOR TODAY ARE: ....

WHO IS THE AUTHOR - DR BRENDA HATTINGH?

Dr. Brenda Hattingh is an international inspirational speaker, leadership coach and mentor, and business, corporate, and leadership consultant. Brenda invests her time in using personal and organisational power and success potential encoded as our unique DNA blueprint. This is a global first in personal and organisational training and development.

Brenda is committed to the development of a new level of consciousness with an awareness of the value of authentic living and leading. She focuses on assisting people, teams, companies, and organisations – who are willing to bring their *best self* to the table.

As an author, Brenda brings to the table cutting edge information, books, and training courses that include topics *like Power Intelligence – the intelligence of the future*, *New Success DNA*, and *New Leadership DNA*. She is Director of the *Power Intelligence Academy* and *The Academy for Authentic Leaders*. Brenda is also the *CEO of the Centre for Power Intelligence*

As an innovator, Brenda is committed to the development of a new generation of successful, innovative, inspired, thinkers and leaders. She speaks at events and conferences, presents workshops nationally and internationally, lectures at various universities, and has published various books.

Her work is featured on TEDx Talks as Brenda introduces the next season of personal development and leadership training that includes tapping into your DNA-blueprint. Brenda is also the recipient of various awards including the *Professional Businesswoman of the Year Award.*

ENROLL FOR A PERSONAL 5-WEEK COURSE.

Title: LEARNING TO COACH YOURSELF TO ULTIMATE SUCCESS

This will be one of the best investments you have ever made.

Background

Times have changed and we need to think on our feet. You can only be super successful and flourish if you know how to coach yourself and manage your inner dialogue. Very few people, especially leaders, know how to do this.

At the moment, we are also experiencing a genetic migration. Humanity is going through a transformation, right down to a DNA level. This means we also need to learn how to activate our DNA success-blueprint. The information on how to do this is now available.

Contact us if you would first like to book a free session

What will you learn?

In this beginner course of *Learning to Coach Yourself*, which runs over five weeks, you will learn:

- Who your real-me is and what your personal purpose is
- How to tap into and activate your DNA success-blueprint
- How to master your inner dynamics and create affluence
- How to create the next level of success and happiness
- How to overcome inner blockages and pitfalls
- To understand the psychology of money and affluence
- To understand the science and psychology of real success
- How to become an authentic leader and influencer
- How to create health, wealth, and happiness that benefits everyone
- And much more…

What will you receive:

- E-book 1. Coaching yourself to ultimate success. Who coaches who?
- E-book 2: Authentic living and leading. What is it and how to develop it
- Your personal workbook for your notes
- Five one-on-one personal coaching sessions via Skype, Zoom, or WhatsApp with Dr. Brenda Hattingh.
- Three DNA-healing sessions
- A plan of action/map for the next season of your life.

Books available on www.amazon.com/books

Who should invest in this course?

Everyone who wants to move forward and create their best life. This includes people like you and me, leaders, teachers, parents, business-persons, couples …

How to book your *Course. Learning to coach yourself?*

Send an email to info@powerintelligence.net. We will send all the necessary information to your inbox.

See our website: http://www.brendahattingh.com

BOOK DR BRENDA HATTINGH AS SPEAKER

To book Dr. Brenda Hattingh as an exciting, entertaining, and inspirational speaker for your next event, or conference and training session, contact us by sending an email to:

Email: info@powerintelligence.net

See website: http://www.brendahattingh.com

ooo0ooo

BOOK DR BRENDA FOR LEADERSHIP TRAINING

Email us: info@powerintelligence.net

ooo0ooo

THE POWER INTELLIGENCE LEADERSHIP ACADEMY

See the courses currently available at the Power Intelligence Leadership academy

Website: https://power-intelligence-leadership-academy.teachable.com

ooo0ooo

CURING CORRUPTION

Corruption is one of the worst pandemics of our time. Corruption is in essence a mental-health issue and should be treated as such. Unfortunately, current strategies are failing because they don't address the fundamental root cause of corruption.

In the two books below, you will find all the necessary information for you to take in your place as part of the solution to the corruption pandemic.

Books available: www.amazon.com/author/brendahattingh

ooo0ooo

AUTHENTIC LEADERS IN ACTION

The world is in chaos and dire need of real, authentic leaders. Some people are awaking and are not afraid to stand up, take in their place, bring peace, build bridges, create a new vision of the future, and shine in their own unique way. These are our authentic leaders.

Such a man was Nelson Mandela.

We accelerate our own awakening, growth, and development by learning from those who went before us.

A course, *Ten lessons from Nelson Mandela…,* is available from https://power-intelligence-leadership-academy.teachable.com. Below you find two books with life-lessons from this iconic leader

. Available from. Amazon.com/author/brendahattingh

REFERENCES

[1] Hattingh, Brenda. (2020). *Authentic leadership. Humanity's leap to authenticity. Where do you stand?* Currency Communications. Johannesburg.

[2] Hattingh, Brenda. (2020). *The Authentic Self. Who am I/* Currency Communications: Johannesburg.

[3] Hattingh, Brenda. (2012. b). *Power Intelligence: Mastering your miracle mind. Currency Communications: Johannesburg.*

[4] Hattingh, Brenda. (2020). *The Authentic Self. Coaching yourself to ultimate success.* Currency Communications. Johannesburg.

[5] Hattingh, Brenda. (2020). *Authentic living. Discovering your DNA success-blueprint.* Currency Communications. Johannesburg.

[6] See website: http://en.wikipedia.org/wiki/Soul

[7] Carl Jung used the term *principium individuationis,* or principle of *individuation.* This describes how a thing is identified from other things.
See website: http://org/wiki/Individuation

[8] Planes of existence: In esoteric cosmology, a *'plane',* other than the physical plane is conceived as a subtle state of consciousness that transcends the known physical universe.
See website: http://en.wikipedia.org/wiki/Plane_(esotericism)
See book:
Hattingh, Brenda. (2020). The *Authentic self – Who am I?* Currency Communications: Johannesburg.

[9] See above: Planes.

[10] Cosmic Light that is not visible to the naked eye. Comic light rays are rising according to ASA. See website:
http://science.nasa.gov/science-news/science-atnasa/2009/29sep_cosmicrays/
See the article in *Time magazine*:
Website: http://www.time.com/time/magazine/article/0,9171,991839,00.html

[11] The Love Law of the Universe: Also known as the Christ Law:
See Holy Bible: Mark 12:28-31.
  30. *'Thou shalt love the Lord thy God with all thy heart, and with all thy soul, and with all thy mind, and with all thy strength: this is the first commandment.*
  31. And the second is like, namely this, Thou shalt love thy neighbour as thyself. There is none other commandments greater than these.'

[12] Hattingh, Brenda. (2012. b.) Power Intelligence. Mastering your Miracle Mind. Currency Communications. Johannesburg.

[13] Series; *'Authentic Living and Leading'* Available:
www.amazon.com/author/brendahattingh.

[14] Hattingh, Brenda. (2020*.) Going for Gold. Mining your DNA-blueprint.* Currency Communications. Johannesburg.

[15] The RAS. The Reticular Activating System. AKA, aura, personal space, personal 'bubble'.

[16] Hattingh, Brenda. (2020). *Authentic leadership. Humanity's leap to authenticity. Where do you stand*? Currency Communications. Johannesburg.

[17] Hattingh, Brenda. (2021). *Power Intelligence. The intelligence of the future.* Currency Communications. Johannesburg.

[18] See book. *Power Intelligence. Mastering your miracle mind.* Chapter 7.

[19] See book: *New Success DNA. What you should know and how to activate it.* Books are available on: www.amazon.com/author/brendahattingh

oooOooo